Summer Walk

For my family. Thank you for all of your love and support.

Manufactured in Shenzhen, China, in January 2016 by Toppan

First Edition
20 19 18 17 16   5 4 3 2 1

Published by
Gibbs Smith
P.O. Box 667
Layton, Utah 84041

1.800.835.4993 orders
www.gibbs-smith.com

Gibbs Smith books are printed on either recycled,
100% post-consumer waste, FSC-certified papers or on
paper produced from sustainable PEFC-certified forest/
controlled wood source. Learn more at www.pefc.org.

Library of Congress Cataloging-in-Publication Data

Names: Snow, Virginia Brimhall.
Title: Summer walk / Virginia Brimhall Snow.
Description: First edition. | Layton, Utah: Gibbs Smith,
2016. | Summary: "Ramble through the woods, as you join
Grammy and her favorite grandkids on a summer walk.
Illustrations and rhymes will guide readers as they learn to
identify twenty-four different insects. At day's end, discover
how to create a caterpillar habitat"– Provided by publisher.
Identifiers: LCCN 2015029223 | ISBN 9781423642152
Subjects: | CYAC: Stories in rhyme. | Insects-Fiction.
| Summer–Fiction.|Grandmothers–Fiction.
Classification: LCC PZ8.3.S674144 Su 2016 | DDC [E]–dc23
LC record available at http://lccn.loc.gov/2015029223

Summer Walk

VIRGINIA BRIMHALL SNOW

GIBBS SMITH
TO ENRICH AND INSPIRE HUMANKIND

KATYDID

I visited my Grammy
one sunny summer day.

As we walked along,
I spied a ladybug by the way.

LADYBUG

PRAYING MANTIS

PILL BUG

I showed Grammy a pill bug
curled up in my hand.

Soon he uncurled
and crawled back to the sand.

DRAGONFLY

Fluffy white clouds
made shapes in the sky:

A dragon, a sailboat,
and a pony—oh my.

PLANTHOPPER

BUTTERFLY

I danced with a butterfly
with blue speckled wings.

"She started as a small egg
on a leaf in the spring."

CATERPILLAR

"From the egg hatched a caterpillar,
  it munched lots of leaves.

"Then," Grammy said,
  "a green chrysalis she weaved."

CHRYSALIS

SWALLOWTAIL

"Inside her tiny home,
a great change was made.

She came out as a butterfly;
on soft breezes she played."

STINK BUG

WATER STRIDER

GRASSHOPPER

I splashed in a stream,
found bugs walking there.

Out jumped a grasshopper—
he gave me a scare!

WALKING STICK

I kicked stones and sticks,
"Wait, that one's alive.

It's camouflaged,"
Grammy told me.
"That's how they survive."

BOXELDER
BUG

"Bugs' bones are on the outside; our bones are in.

See, this red spotted beetle has hard, shiny skin."

SNAIL

BEETLE

CICADA

ANT

The sun was quite warm,
so I rested in the shade,

Watched little insects,
and sipped lemonade.

MOSQUITO

A buzzing mosquito landed
weightless on my arm.

Slap! Now he's gone and
will do no more harm.

LACEWING

HONEY BEE

FIREFLY

We were almost home
when the sunset blazed red.

"Grammy, can we catch fireflies
before we go to bed?"

CRICKET

MOTH

Crickets chirped us a song
as we closed our day.

"Goodbye all you bugs,
I wish that I could stay."

CLOUD SHAPES PICTURE

- Construction paper

- Cotton balls

- Glue

- Toothpicks for spreading glue (optional)

DIRECTIONS:

- Gather all of the materials on a table.

- Choose a colored paper. For a daytime picture, try using a blue paper. Orange paper can look like a sunset, and pink is great for a sunrise.

- For thin, wispy clouds (cirrus), stretch a cotton ball out until you can see through it. Spread some glue on the paper, using a toothpick if you want, and pat the cotton cloud in place.

- For fat rain clouds (cumulus), stretch a cotton ball just a little and glue it down. Then slightly stretch one or more cotton balls and glue them next to the first one or on top of it.

- Use your imagination to make lots of unique shapes with the cotton ball clouds.

HATCHING BUTTERFLIES

YOU WILL NEED:

- A large glass mason jar with lid and ring

- Hammer and nail

- Paper towels

- Small stick that will fit in the jar

- Caterpillar

- Milkweed leaves for monarch caterpillar

  OR

- Parsley leaves for swallowtail caterpillar

DIRECTIONS:

- With the help of an adult, use the hammer and nail to punch a few holes in the lid.

- Put a paper towel in the bottom of the jar. (This makes it easier to clean up the caterpillar poop.)

- Put a stick in the jar, propped against the side. This gives the caterpillar something to hang its chrysalis from.

- To find a monarch caterpillar, look on milkweed plants. Look on parsley plants for a swallowtail caterpillar. When you find a caterpillar, pick the stalk of the plant it is on and put both in the jar.

- Caterpillars get the water they need from the plants they eat. Take good care of your caterpillar by giving it a fresh stalk of leaves every day, and throw away the old leaves. They are very picky about their food, so only feed them the type of leaves you found them on. Also change the paper towel in the bottom often to help them stay healthy.

- In a few days, the fat caterpillar will spin a chrysalis and rest inside while it turns into a butterfly. It might not choose the stick you put in to hang from. That's okay. The chrysalis will change color as the butterfly forms and gets close to coming out. Check it often.

- When the butterfly emerges from the chrysalis, take it outside and watch while it stretches its wings and then flies away. Be careful not to touch the wings, because they are fragile.

- If you do not live where you can find caterpillars, commercial butterfly raising kits are available with coupons to purchase live caterpillars and food.

Insect Fun Facts

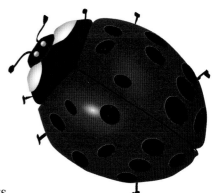

1. Insects have six legs, and sometimes they have wings.

2. Ladybugs are harmless to people. They eat bugs that are bad for plants.

3. Crickets chirp by rubbing their wings together. They rub them faster when it is hot.

4. Honey bees gather nectar from flowers. They tell other bees in the hive where flowers are with a special waggle dance. Most honey bees are female.

5. Katydids and walking sticks are two insects that look a lot like things around them. This is called camouflage. It helps to keep them safe.

6. Water striders have special feet and very long legs that make it possible for them to walk on water. They prefer quiet water, like that in ponds.

7. Some kinds of butterflies migrate from places that are cold in the winter to warmer climates. The next spring, they fly back.

8. One type of cicada lives underground for seventeen years before it emerges as an adult insect.

9. The firefly's glow is caused by a chemical reaction inside of them. The light does not generate heat.

10. Dragonflies can be found in a variety of colors, including blue, green, gold, red, pink, and purple.

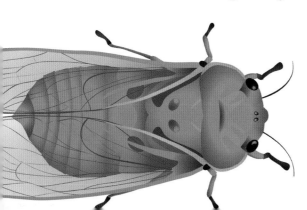